DESERT RACERS

TRACY NELSON MAURER

Rourke
Publishing LLC
Vero Beach, Florida 32964

www.rourkepublishing.com

Project Assistance
Ed Newman, AMSOIL INC.

Also, the author extends appreciation to Stephen Razo (BLM), Mike Maurer, and Kendall and Lois M. Nelson.
Special thanks to desertracing.com

Photo Credits: All photos © desertracing.com except cover © Trackside Photo and page 41 © www.4wheelers.com

Title page: Professional desert races can cover anywhere from 93 miles (150 km) for the SCORE Laughlin Desert Challenge in Nevada to 6,000 miles (9656 km) for the rugged Dakar Rally across North Africa.

Editor: Frank Sloan

Cover and page design: Nicola Stratford

Notice: The publisher recognizes that some words, model names, and designations mentioned herein are the property of the trademark holder. We use them for identification purposes only. This is not an official publication.

Library of Congress Cataloging-in-Publication Data

Maurer, Tracy, 1965-
   Desert racers / Tracy Nelson Maurer.
       p. cm. -- (Roaring rides)
Summary: Discusses the history and current popularity of four-wheel drive vehicles, as well as how they are used in desert racing around the world.
Includes bibliographical references and index.
   ISBN 1-58952-746-1 (hardcover)
   1. Off-road vehicles--Juvenile literature. 2. Four-wheel drive trucks--Juvenile literature. 3. All terrain vehicle racing--Juvenile literature. [1. Off-road vehicles. 2. Four-wheel drive trucks. 3. Trucks. 4. All terrain vehicle racing.] I. Title: Four by four desert trucks. II. Title. III. Series.
   TL230.15.M38 2003
   629.22'042--dc21

                                                                2003009767

Ppk 1-58952-922-7

Printed in the USA

w/w

DESERT RACERS
TABLE OF CONTENTS

The gnarled and uncertain landscape pushes desert racers and their machines to their limits.

CHAPTER ONE

4-BYS

Beautiful but brutally dry deserts don't exactly roll out the red carpet for visitors. Rock-spiked roads, shifty sand flats, feisty hills, jagged turns, yawning mud bogs, flash floods, and other assorted **hazards** replace welcome mats.

Desert racers don't complain. The worst of the desert makes the best challenge for these hardcore drivers! They seek the harsh, sand-whipped playgrounds nearly every weekend to test themselves and their vehicles.

A HUGE SPORT

Today in America, 4x4 (say: four-by-four) cars, trucks, vans, and sport-utility vehicles (SUVs) fill city streets and rural garages. People like the added power, **traction**, and control that four-wheel drive gives them.

A two-wheel drive car or truck uses only the front two wheels (front-wheel drive) or back two wheels (rear-wheel drive) for power. A 4x4, or "4-by," puts all four wheels into the effort— pulling a boat, charging through snow, or racing off-road.

The modern off-road 4-by traces its history to World War II. The United States military used quarter-ton and three-quarter-ton trucks equipped with four-wheel drive to haul supplies and soldiers to battlefields. These rigs blazed trails in some nasty places.

The power of a 4x4 is handy for brutal off-road terrain. However, many desert racing vehicles use two-wheel drive.

HUMBLE BEASTS

In time, truck and car manufacturers offered 4x4s for civilians. Today, those early Ford Broncos, Dodge Rams, and other favorites still conquer off-road challenges. Some official desert races offer divisions for the 4x4 classics.

Beefy 4x4s zoomed in popularity when manufacturers softened the stiff ride and improved the handling. Leather seats, deluxe stereos, and other fancy options tamed the beasts.

Although these humbled 4x4 grocery-getters rarely venture off the pavement except perhaps to park on the grass at the soccer field, they're still fairly well built to hit the dusty trail.

Most 4x4s use automatic **transmissions**. Many city-slickers joined the 4x4 parade when manufacturers replaced manual transmissions with automatics—no more manually shifting gears and working the clutch.

Drivers set up their cabs with the equipment that works best for them— nothing too fancy!

Drivers shift down to lower gears to gain more power when they climb hills like this one.

ALL HANDS AND FEET

Manual transmissions keep the driver's hands and feet busy. The driver starts in neutral (no gears engaged) with the left foot holding the clutch pedal to the floorboard. The driver's right hand moves the gear-shifting lever into first gear. The left hand steers.

The tricky part? The driver gives the vehicle gas by gently pushing down the **accelerator** pedal with the right foot. At the same time, the left foot eases out the clutch pedal. First-timers kill their engines a lot before they lurch forward enough to try second gear.

Desert drivers like to shift into lower gears for more power in tough spots. Higher gears offer less power but more speed. Think of the gears on a ten-speed bicycle. The bike rider drops down to the smaller, lower gears for more power when pedaling up a hill. Then the rider shifts to the larger, higher gears for more speed on the flat stretches.

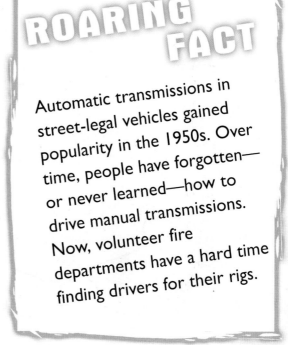

ROARING FACT

Automatic transmissions in street-legal vehicles gained popularity in the 1950s. Over time, people have forgotten—or never learned—how to drive manual transmissions. Now, volunteer fire departments have a hard time finding drivers for their rigs.

Drivers set up their trucks mainly for power. The 4x4 truck drivers adjust the gears inside the pumpkin-shaped **differential** boxes at the front and rear under the truck to give their large tires more power.

In desert racing, power often wins over speed. Without enough power, a truck can bog down in sand or mud. It might balk at a steep climb.

"You can't win unless you finish," the racers say.

A winning racer looks for every opportunity to hammer a flat stretch with a burst of speed.

DESERT RACERS

CHAPTER TWO

READY TO ROCK

Racers might churn across open flats at more than 100 miles (160 km) per hour, leap off small cliffs, chop across the tops of hard-packed sand ripples called whoops, or plod up bare rock. **Endurance** events that last for days really abuse the vehicles.

Mile after mile, drivers must stay focused to avoid crashes, rollovers, and other dangerous speed bumps along the way— in daylight or darkness. Careful preparation before the race often decides which racers cross the finish line.

BUILDING A BETTER TRUCK

Professional teams carefully build their trucks from the ground up. For speed, they want lightweight and sleek designs. For strength, they want heavy-duty construction. Bolt by bolt, hose by hose, and gear by gear, they fine-tune the machine for desert conditions.

Before a big race, the team often tears down the entire vehicle and rebuilds certain parts. Mechanics check the brakes, power steering, and electrical system. Specialists might test the engine, transmission, and **suspension system** before race day, too.

Racing teams use special **lubricants** to help their engines tolerate the desert's extreme conditions, especially during the long-distance runs.

Every change, or modification, must meet the race circuit's strict rules. A **sanctioning** organization sets the exact measurements, equipment list, and other rules for each racing class, or division. Judges may inspect the vehicles before, during, and after the race. They can send the rule-breakers home.

ROARING FACT

Race officials use "DNF" in the results to mean "did not finish." In desert racing, the officials feel proud when 60 percent—more than half—actually finish a race.

A team unloads its rebuilt truck. The power-hungry machine is ready to race!

RIDING HIGH

Professional teams try to select tires for the conditions they expect on the desert course. Specialized sand tires with paddle-like lugs might float on top off the sand better than deeply grooved rock-climbing tires. Often, professional racing tires are not legal to drive on the street.

Bigger tires cover more territory each time they spin around than smaller, normal tires do. These tires deliver more traction, too. They also help lift the vehicle higher off the ground for greater **clearance**.

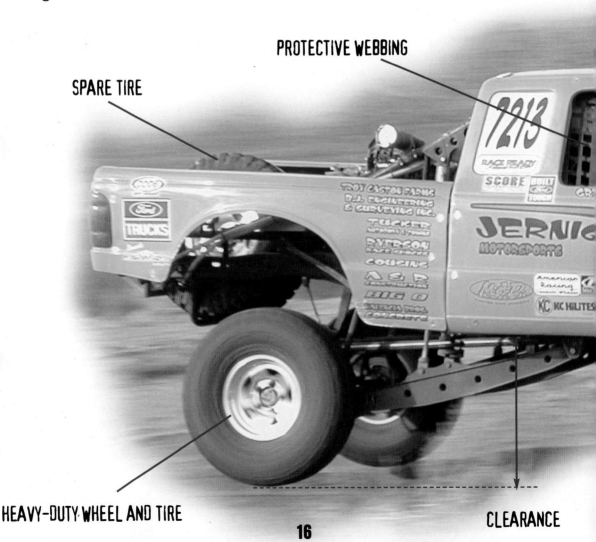

PROTECTIVE WEBBING

SPARE TIRE

HEAVY-DUTY WHEEL AND TIRE

CLEARANCE

Clearance allows the truck to pass over boulders, stumps, and other metal-munchers. The suspension system also lets each wheel travel up and over rocks without jamming the big tire into the fender or belly of the truck.

Sometimes the frame needs a boost, too. Lifts, or blocks, under the frame help to keep the body from rubbing on the oversized tires.

CAB WITH INTERNAL ROLL-CAGE

BRUSH GUARD WITH FOG LIGHTS

HEAVY-DUTY SUSPENSION SYSTEM AND LIFTS

AIRING DOWN

Powdery silt or shifty sand causes traction trouble for tires. Teams look at how much rubber stands on the ground—the tire's footprint. A larger footprint resists sinking into sand, just like a larger rubber raft floats a load better than a tiny one.

To make a larger footprint, the teams let air out of each tire. An air pressure **gauge** checks that all four tires have the same pressure per square inch, or psi.

Full tires measure a greater distance around than under-inflated tires (just like a full balloon is a lot rounder than an empty one). The engine uses less energy pushing the smaller diameters around.

Still, airing down the tires takes skillful driving. The rig loses clearance. Rolling on the puffs of air, the wheel rims mangle easily. Under-inflated tires build up heat if the truck gains speed, too. Wise drivers refill the tires before they hit the high-speed flat stretches.

Racers carry two spare tires. They may air-down the tires during the race to gain traction. Normal street tires might have 35 psi. Some endurance racers flatten their tires down to as little as 3 psi!

Desert racing is not kind to tires. Rough landings and jagged rocks can flatten them.

Race trucks use strong webbed nets on the driver and passenger windows. Other safety features include spark-arrestors or muffler systems directed away from the vehicles.

SAFETY ALL AROUND

Racing rules require teams to install many safety features, such as net windows instead of breakable glass. Each truck must have a rollbar made of steel tubing, too. This sturdy cage guards the driver if the truck crashes.

Off-road fires pose a serious safety risk, since firefighters may not be able to reach a burning vehicle quickly—or at all. Professional race teams must install specially designed fuel cells, or gas tanks, in the vehicles. These rubber-coated metal tanks have fire-resistant plastic liners filled with baffles, or sets of divider walls, to keep gasoline from sloshing or exploding.

A firewall between the engine and the cab protects the driver from heat and flames if the truck catches on fire. To protect the desert habitat from fire, the trucks also use government-approved spark-arrestors or muffler systems. Drivers and their pit crews keep fire extinguishers handy, too.

ROARING FACT

Anyone traveling in the desert should carry a weatherproof first-aid kit with bandages, antiseptic, eye dressings, and maybe a wire splint. Wise desert visitors pack a survival kit, too, with extra goggles, a bandana, sun block, whip, paddles, water, firewood, tow strap, and plenty of gasoline. Most important, they bring lots of common sense.

SMART SAFETY GEAR

Because of the fire risks, drivers wear double-layered fire-retardant jumpsuits, gloves, socks, and shoes. Some drivers write their blood type and other medical information on their suits, just in case they need emergency care.

All drivers wear safety-rated helmets. Most professionals wear neck braces beneath the helmet, too. Like the helmet, the neck brace uses fire-resistant materials. These U-shaped cushions keep the drivers' heads from jiggling when their trucks bounce across whoops or take hard landings off dunes.

Drivers sit in their cabs behind solid windshields, but they still carry shatter-resistant goggles or wear helmet visors. Gritty sand blows into the cab and seems to be everywhere. It settles in their noses and mouths, too. Some drivers wear sand masks or scarves to filter the sand. Still, they crunch and grind at least a little sand with every meal!

ROARING FACT

The Best In The Desert Racing Association recommends that racers take out their removable dentures, if they use them, during events. The false teeth could become choking hazards on those bone-rattling courses.

Even when changing a tire under the blazing desert sun, racers must wear full racing suits and helmets for safety. A passing vehicle could kick up rocks or spin off broken parts.

STUBS AND STICKERS

Before the race, each driver receives a "stuck stub" that must stay in the vehicle unless the driver needs help. Then another racer can pick up the stub and deliver it to a race judge.

Each driver must also carry glow sticks, flashlights, reflectors, and other ways to signal. The driver packs a first-aid kit, at least one day of survival food, and plenty of water, too.

If a driver and rig pass all of the pre-race safety checks, the race officials slap an inspection sticker on the vehicle. The racer may also wear an armband that shows he or she is approved to run the course.

A passing racer picked up this driver's stuck stub, and his teammates came to the rescue.

CHAPTER THREE

THE LONG HAUL

Desert racing for hundreds of miles has plenty of exciting moments, but drivers fight **fatigue** just the same. Boredom creeps up on the long stretches where cacti and lizards outnumber cheering fans.

Professionals work out to build their **stamina** and strength. They pump up their upper-body muscles. The extra power helps them to wrangle the steering wheel through twisting routes and quickly dig out their stuck trucks. Flabby muscles may cramp after holding the same position mile after mile.

DOUBLE DESERT CREWS

Most long-distance races split the racing duties between two drivers. Even highly skilled and talented driving teams would be lost without their pit crews and chase teams.

Pit crews stake out positions along the way, often about 50 miles (80 km) apart. Quick pit stops can win or lose a race.

Judges watch to see that the pit crews follow the rules. Pit crews can't drive the wrong way on the course to go back to fix a rig. They can only wait for their drivers to come to them.

Chase crews follow their racers with water, food, clothes, and other necessities for the drivers.

The Core Team Members

Owner – Owns the vehicle, and may provide financial support

Drivers – Take turns driving the vehicle; they usually fix it, too

Pit crew – Service the car at checkpoints and offer food and water to the drivers

Chase crew – Follow the racing rig with supplies

Sponsors – Support the team by paying to advertise on the race vehicle

A pit crew quickly tends to its truck at a checkpoint. The crew must follow the rules or the judges could send the team home.

Champion Focus:
Enduro Racing's Top Desert Duo

Rumbling across the desert, one desert duo leaves a trail of shattered speed records along the way. Team Manager/Co-driver Dave Ashley and Co-Driver Dan Smith push their Ford trucks to the limit for Enduro Racing. Both drivers started racing on motorcycles and switched to four wheels later in their careers. This talented off-road pair stays focused on winning. Their trophies prove it!

Dave Ashley
Birthday: April 5, 1957
Height: 6' 0" (1.82 m)
Weight: 195 lbs (88.5 kg)
Home: Riverside, California
Married
Started racing trucks: 1979
Race Wins: Baja 2000, Baja 1000 (8 times), 25 other events
Season Champ: 12 times, various SCORE and Best-in-the Desert classes

Dan Smith
Birthday: Nov. 23, 1963
Height: 5' 11" (1.8 m)
Weight: 185 lbs (83.9 kg)
Home: Riverside, California
Married
Started racing trucks: 1991 (Rookie of the Year)
Race wins: Baja 2000, Baja 1000 (7 times), 50 other events
Season Champ: 15 times, various competitions

Racers use GPS to plan their routes during long races like the Baja 1000.

BAJA, BABY!

Since 1967, the Baja 1000 in Mexico has become the ultimate off-road challenge for long-distance desert racers. Sanctioned by SCORE International of California, this world-famous race features slightly more than 1,000 miles (1,600 km) of gritty dust, bumpy gravel, and tire-piercing rocks mixed with heat, fumes, and rowdy crowds.

Most teams "pre-run" or drive the entire course a week before the race. The teams program their GPS (global positioning satellite) systems along the way. They enter data about hazards, legal shortcuts, or crowd zones. They also note the checkpoints.

Events held in the United States usually do not permit teams to pre-run race courses due to environmental concerns.

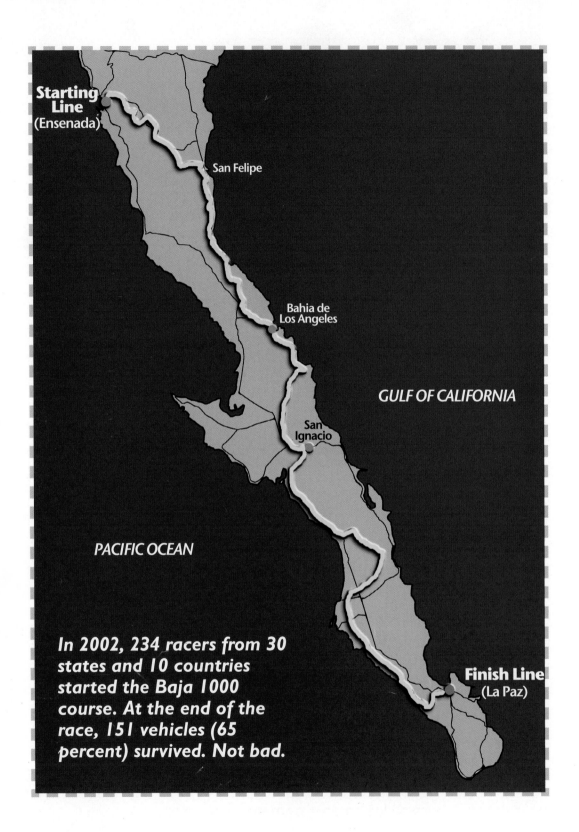

Starting Line (Ensenada)

San Felipe

Bahia de Los Angeles

GULF OF CALIFORNIA

San Ignacio

PACIFIC OCEAN

Finish Line (La Paz)

In 2002, 234 racers from 30 states and 10 countries started the Baja 1000 course. At the end of the race, 151 vehicles (65 percent) survived. Not bad.

POINT TO POINT

The SCORE Baja 1000 starts and ends in different places. It's called a point-to-point race. The excitement kicks off in Ensenada, a city on the peninsula's Pacific Ocean side. Sandy rooster tails blast from trucks, cars, motorcycles, and All-Terrain Vehicles (ATVs) as they charge over the starting line.

Racers rip through town and burst into the open country where speeds top 100 miles (161 km) per hour. They cross the finish line in the southern city of La Paz.

Many races like the Baja 1000 use an elapsed-time format. The official clock begins ticking when the first vehicle roars over the start line. When a certain number of hours have passed—40 hours for the Baja 1000—the race stops. Any drivers who have not crossed the finish line before the elapsed time will receive a big DNF (Did Not Finish).

ROARING FACT

Desert race fans flock to the legendary Coco's Corner during events. Located between Gonzaga and Bahia de los Angeles in Mexico, Coco's Corner serves beverages and offers a handy repair shop. More than a few desert adventurers have been rescued courtesy of Coco, the owner.

For some professional racers, the Baja 1000 becomes a practice run for the brutal Dakar Rally. For other racers, the Baja 1000 is all the challenge they ever want to tackle!

DAKAR DAREDEVILS

Instead of point-to-point, a long-distance course may also follow a loop design that starts and finishes in the same place. The brutal 6,000-mile (9,656-km) Dakar Rally across North Africa uses both loops and point-to-point sections, sometimes taking 21 days to finish.

When it began in the late 1970s, this motor marathon started in Paris and ended in Dakar on Africa's west coast.

Now the route changes nearly every year, mainly to avoid political messes, civil wars, and other threats. Even then, trouble sneaks up. In 2003, organizers airlifted some 525 vehicles from one country to another, bypassing possible ambush sites discovered during the event.

The Dakar Rally features three major classes, including cars, motorcycles, and trucks—not pick-ups but ten-ton hulks that double as support vehicles for the cars and bikes. More than 600 drivers might start a race. Maybe half of the daredevils finish.

ROARING FACT

Dehydration, or lack of water for the body, can really ruin a driver's day. Everyone in the desert, including drivers, pit crew, judges, and fans, must drink plenty of water to stay healthy. Of course, drivers also want to avoid potty breaks. A few racers wear catheters, bladder drainage tubes temporarily set in their privates. S-q-u-i-r-r-r-m!

Many desert races include classes for motorcycles.

ROARING FACT

The Dakar Rally requires careful planning to run through several countries. Organizers use more than 20 aircraft and 40 vehicles for safety and medical equipment, food, maintenance, supplies, and press coverage.

DESERT RACERS

CHAPTER FOUR

ROOM TO REV

Scientists figure that deserts cover about one fifth of the planet. The world's largest desert, the Sahara in North Africa, covers about 3.5 million square miles (9.06 sq km). That's close to the same size as the entire United States!

North America's four deserts—Chihuahuan, Great Basin, Mojave, and Sonoran—touch roughly 478,000 square miles (1,237,924 sq km) in the western and southern United States and parts of Mexico. Mexico's Baja Peninsula lies in the Sonoran Desert.

SAND RATS AND DUNERS

Every race attracts crowds that friends call "sand rats." Fans often pitch camps along the race route. Some arrive in specially built recreational vehicles (RVs) that combine a cab for driving, an area for sleeping and eating, and a storage area for ATVs, bikes, or even trucks.

Many families don't race their vehicles. They just play in the desert. These "duners" rumble across their favorite off-highway area every weekend, especially when the season starts in late October. Temperatures cool down then.

Families enjoy the racing action together.

Thousands of acres of public desert lands are closed to off-road driving. Some groups favor completely banning desert riding. They worry about pollution. They say motorsports destroy the plant and animal habitats.

Other groups like the American Sand Association (ASA) work to preserve public lands for off-road sports. They also promote safe and responsible off-road driving.

RIDE WITH PRIDE

Wise duners take pride in the places where they play. They take care of desert habitats. Some have joined the ASA "Checkered Flag" movement to support law enforcement in the dunes.

Rules to Remember:
- Maintain off-road vehicles and top off the gas tank. Sand driving uses more gas than pavement.
- Pack safety, survival, and repair supplies.
- Check with local authorities for closures. Check the weather forecasts.
- Never ride alone. Stay with the vehicle if it gets stuck—rescuers see the vehicle easier than a person.
- Fly a red or orange safety flag on an 8-foot (2.4-m) mast.
- Watch the speed!
- No fires, no glass containers.
- Never drink alcohol and drive—including an off-road vehicle.
- Leave no garbage behind.

ROARING FACT

WE FLY IT AND LIVE BY IT!
TRASH:
WE pack it in and WE pack it out
ENFORCEMENT:
WE live by the rules
WE support all law enforcement
    at the dunes
WE report major infractions
RESPECT FOR OTHER PEOPLE,
SAFETY AND THE
ENVIRONMENT:
WE act in a responsible manner

Courtesy of the American Sand Association and supported by the Bureau of Land Management

DESERT RACERS

CHAPTER FIVE

MORE OFF-ROAD RIDES

Desert motor sports gain fans all the time. Today, off-road vehicles include more than 4x4 trucks. Hummers, VW Bugs, open-wheel sand cars, dune buggies, Jeeps, dirt bikes, and ATVs charge through the desert. They tackle **obstacle** courses, crawl up rocks, and jump dunes.

Professionals race these other types of vehicles, too. Like 4x4 trucks, the rigs must be tuned for the desert. Fixing a Jeep to race can cost anywhere from $10,000 to $15,000.

ROCK ROVERS

Rock crawling has become especially popular with the 4x4 crowd in recent years. Many traditional off-road racers have switched to this up-and-coming (pun intended) sport.

Men and women drive radical rigs with amazing suspension systems over, between, and around massive boulders and ravines. The heavy-duty shock absorbers let the wheels move in different directions without breaking off. Some rigs look like bulked-up dune buggies. They use oversized tires like other desert racers.

Drivers look for the best line, or route, through the rocky course. Attacking at an angle instead of straight-on might make the difference between finishing or not. Rollovers happen a lot. Spotters work the winches to pull the rigs up over the tricky spots.

ROARING FACT

Rock crawling organizations continue to form across the United States. Many sanctioned events take place in the western states, but look for new "crawls" soon in the eastern regions.

The extreme sport of rock crawling gains new fans all the time.

SPONSOR SUPPORT

Desert racing takes money, even at the amateur level. Every vehicle at the starting line might sport thousands of dollars in parts, mechanical work, and repairs. That's not counting travel expenses, extra insurance, gasoline, licenses, or race entry fees.

Race organizers try to keep costs down for participants to help their sport grow. To help lower the costs of running a race, the organizers work with advertisers and sponsors.

Racers pour a lot of money into their sport. Winning helps attract sponsors to fund the team's effort—sponsors pay to advertise on the race vehicle.

A few teams have signed with factory sponsors such as Ford Motor Company and Honda. The drivers, vehicles, pit crews, and chase teams show the sponsor logos any time they can—they're moving billboards for the companies.

Some sponsors offer **contingency** prizes in addition to the cash that drivers take home for winning. Usually, the winner must have a logo from that sponsor on his or her vehicle to claim a contingency prize. Protruck Racing now offers winning racers more than $150,000 in contingency cash and products.

DESERT FANS

Desert motor sports, like 4x4 racing, often become the highlight of camping trips for many families. Some people volunteer to help at events or they work on the rigs that run in the races. Most families simply go to cheer for their favorite teams. Then they rev up their own machines for fun in the sun.

Not everyone races in the desert. People enjoy sightseeing, hiking, horseback riding, biking, and many other activities.

Check out the local library for more information on deserts and desert racing. Many books, magazines, and videos cover the sport. The Internet also offers many updated Web sites.

Further Reading

4-Wheel Freedom: The Art of Off-Road Driving by Brad DeLong. Paladin Press, Boulder, CO (updated edition), 2000.

Petersen's 4Wheel & Off-Road Magazine
www.4wheeloffroad.com

Web Sites

American Sand Association
http://www.americansandassociation.org/

Best in the Desert
http://www.bitd.com/

CORR (Championship Off-Road Racing)
http://www.corracing.com

Desert USA
http://www.desertusa.com/who/du_maps.html

DesertRacing.com
http://www.desertracing.com

Online off-road resource
http://www.off-road.com/

SCORE International
http://www.score-international.com

S.N.O.R.E. (Southern Nevada Off-Road Enthusiasts)
http://www.Go-Desert.com

U.S. Department of the Interior
Bureau of Land Management, California Desert District
http://www.ca.blm.gov/faqs.html
http://www.californiadesert.gov/

Glossary

accelerator (ak SELL ah ray tur) — in vehicles, the pedal device that controls the speed

clearance (KLEER ahs) — in vehicles, the space between the ground and the frame

contingency (kahn TIN jen s ee) — in racing, a contingency prize is a bonus awarded to the race winner if the winner meets certain rules, such as displaying the sponsor's logo

differential (diff ah REN shul) — a gear device that allows two or more shafts to spin at different speeds

endurance (en DUHR ahns) — power or strength to keep going or continue for a long time or distance

fatigue (fah TEEGH) — feeling weary, tired, or weak

gauge (GAYJ) — a device that shows a standard measurement, such as the pressure per square inch, called psi, in an air pressure gauge

hazards (HAZ urdz) — dangers or risks; things that are not safe

lubricants (LOO bri kents) — oil or grease that reduces friction, rubbing, or grinding between working mechanical parts

obstacle (OB stah kull) — something that stands in the way or blocks a path

sanction (SANGK shun) — to approve or to allow; to make rules

stamina (STAM ah nah) — strength and power to keep going, to continue

suspension system (sah SPEN shun SISS tihm) — in vehicles, the system of shock absorbers, springs, and other parts between the wheel and frame designed to create a smooth ride and better control

traction (TRAK shun) — sticking or gripping to a surface

transmission (trans MISH un) — in vehicles, the unit of gears that allows the engine's power to move the wheels

Index

About The Author

Tracy Nelson Maurer specializes in nonfiction and business writing. Her most recently published children's books include the RadSports series, also from Rourke Publishing LLC. Tracy lives with her husband Mike and two children near Minneapolis, Minnesota.